#Goals

A Quick Introduction	3
Lesson 1: Hierarchy of Goals	4
Lesson 2: The Mile	9
Lesson 3: Challenges in the Mile	13
Lesson 4: Discouragement of Distance	19
Lesson 5: Breaking Down the Mile (Overview)	23
Lesson 6: Breaking Down the Mile (Defining It)	27
Lesson 7: Breaking Down the Mile (Creating Steps)	31
Lesson 8: Celebrating Milestones	36
Lesson 9: Complex Miles	40
Lesson 10: Commitment	44
Lesson 11: People and Our Goals	48
Lesson 12: Winning the Day	52

Copyright © 2017 by Chris Capehart
All rights reserved.

ISBN-13: 978-0-9970298-6-4

Updated Edition October 2018
Original Edition November 2017

Published in the United States of America
1 2 3 4 5 6 7 8 9 10

A Quick Introduction

It's time to look at goals differently. To approach them with a fresh perspective that makes achieving them possible.

Is it possible to achieve our goals? Statistics say that only a small percentage of people who set goals will actually accomplish them. But you don't have to be a statistic.

I've spent the majority of my life tackling big goals. From creating millions of dollars in revenue to writing a book. I've gone headfirst into just about every large goal I've ever come up with, and along the way I've learned a few things about setting and achieving them. I write about this in my book *Step*, but wanted to create a tool that would dive even deeper into how we set and achieve goals. This workbook does just that.

This is about you achieving your goals. What is it you want to achieve? Maybe it's an income level, or it could be paying off debt, buying a house, or just being a better parent. Whatever your goal, this course will help you along the path. There's no risk greater than not risking at all. Now is the time for you to equip yourself to achieve your goals. Let's see what's possible together.

How It Works

On the following pages you'll find 12 lessons. Each lesson is followed by a study guide and a page for notes. Read through each lesson and complete the accompanying study guide. Make sure to take a few minutes to jot down any thoughts in the notes section. There's no right or wrong speed to go through the workbook. You can do it all in one day or take a month or two. Go at a pace that works for you.

Each lesson also has a corresponding video lesson that can be accessed as a part of the Intentional Year Video Library. To find out more about the video library, go to ChrisCapehart.co or email us at hello@chriscapehart.co.

Lesson 1: *Hierarchy of Goals*

The history of maps is pretty fascinating. Beginning in Babylon with clay tablets in 2300 BC and moving to 17th, 18th, and 19th century maps, we see accuracy improving and the application of scientific methods. Maps are ever evolving. *Modern* maps really emerged following World War I when aerial photography was integrated into the map-making world, and our modern maps, rich with both ground observations and remote sensing, created a greater sense of understanding for us all.

Just in my lifetime I've seen maps take three major transformations. I remember the first out-of-state road trip I took by myself. I was in high school and a good friend of mine and I were driving from Arkansas to Texas for my brother's wedding. We barely had cell phones and I think GPS was probably only being used by NASA at this point, so we used a *massive* Rand McNally map. It must have been 3 feet by 3 feet. Before we left, we sat down with our parents and they helped us map out the route. Some of you will remember doing this too... We took a highlighter and traced our route along the path, so we didn't veer off course. Fast-forward to a few years later and MapQuest had changed the world. But technology wasn't quite fast enough or good enough for us to use it on our phones, so every trip had to be created before we left home and *printed out*. However, this was a *big* advancement over the massive map, because we didn't have to think as much about where we were going. These days, I use my voice to tell Siri where I want to go and she plots the course and re-routes it for me if there's too much traffic, or if I make a wrong turn—which of course I never do!

The main difference between my first road trip with Rand McNally and the trusty highlighter plotting to my current voice commands with Siri is the amount of brainpower traveling requires. You see, a physical map forces you to learn the road. In fact, I could drive it again from memory after only having traveled it once. But compare that to now. I have good friends that I've visited multiple times, but if I don't put their address in my GPS, I'll never make it to their house. Though I've driven the route a handful of times, I've used almost zero brainpower to navigate my course. The app on my phone took care of that for me.

Why so much about maps? And what does any of this have to do with goals?

A map actually has quite a bit in common with achieving a goal. For instance, you can get in your car and start driving, but *if you don't know where you're going, you'll end up anywhere but not necessarily where you want to be*. However, if you know your destination, you can map a course down to the turn. Think about the turns on your map like the goals along the way to achieving the ultimate story you want for your life, family, business, etc. How do you know what turn to make (goals to set) if you don't know where you're going?

Note: Life Story is a resource I've created to help people create the ultimate story they want for their life, family, and business. If you have trouble knowing what your ultimate purpose in these areas is, check it out.

Statistics say that only a small percentage of people who set goals will achieve them. However, the reason only a small percentage of people achieve their goals is not because it's not possible, but because they don't set goals the right way. If someone told me the majority of people who took road trips didn't successfully get to their destination, I'd think that sounds a bit crazy. Then, I'd probably ask if they used a map. The thought of it not being possible would never cross my mind, because just about anyone with a map should be able to successfully reach their destination 99% of the time... And it's the same with goals, but that map isn't always as clear. I'm going to give you step-by-step instructions on how to stack the odds of achieving your goals in your favor and it starts by having a defined destination.

Sometimes you'll hear me refer to this destination as your Life Story, which could also be translated as "the story you want for your life or business." One of the biggest reasons people quit their goals before they achieve them is because their goals do not have a direct correlation to the story they want to write for their life, family, or business. And if they do, they may not have realized it.

Goals that fit into a larger plan have the highest likelihood of getting achieved. So when setting any goal, we should first ask:

Does this goal take me closer to the story I want for my life, family, business, etc?

If you're setting goals that don't align with a bigger story, you're setting yourself up for failure. Let me give an example from our map analogy. Let's say your ultimate destination is Florida (going to Disney World for the first time and it's been a dream of yours forever) and you're starting in California. About halfway through the trip you find yourself in Dallas, Texas. The map says to head toward Louisiana, but you decide to turn left and go to Minnesota. That's completely the opposite direction of Florida and about halfway to Minnesota you start to wonder what you're doing and then ultimately give up on the trip, turn around, and head back home. I know that sounds crazy, but that left turn is like setting a goal that although there's nothing wrong with it, doesn't help you get to where you ultimately want to be.

We want to set goals that move us closer to our ultimate destination. Consider how a short-term goal can overstep a long-term goal. For example, upgrading your current rental house *now* may fulfill the purpose of gaining extra space, but it may jeopardize the bigger goal of saving more money for a down payment toward owning a home. Here's another example: I want to pay for my daughter's college and I have a plan to do that using a rental property; however, what if I had a desire to start a new business as well, and I decided I would get the startup cash by diverting money from rental property income into the new business?

Well, the goal of getting startup cash may fit into my plan of starting the business, but it messes with my overall life story, which includes paying for my daughter's college. It wouldn't align with my purpose for those properties, and I need to think about it from a big picture before I make a decision.

There are multiple routes to any given destination. Typically, when I plug an address into my GPS it will offer a suggested route, but it lets me see the alternative options as well: *this route is 1 minute slower or 5 minutes faster, this route has tolls, and this one has construction.* Just as with multiple routes, we will have to choose the one the best fits our life. For example, a single mom and recent graduate of college may have the same desire to start their own business. However, the path will look different because their circumstances are different and that's okay.

When it comes to creating goals, don't create them in a vacuum. There should be a hierarchy to the goals we create that will drastically increase our odds of achieving not only the individual goal we're setting, but the most important one as well.

Study Guide: *Hierarchy of Goals*

(Fill in the blanks or answer the questions from this lesson.)

Think about the turns on your map like the _____ along the way to achieving the ultimate story you want for your life, family, business, etc.

Goals that fit into a _____ have the highest likelihood of getting achieved.

Questions You Should Ask of Every Goal

Goal: _____

1. How does this goal fit into the story I want for my life (business, etc.)?
_____.

2. Based on the answer above, should I continue pursuing this goal and why?
_____.

Goal: _____

1. How does this goal fit into the story I want for my life (business, etc.)?
_____.

2. Based on the answer above, should I continue pursuing this goal and why?
_____.

Notes: *Hierarchy of Goals*

Lesson 2: *The Mile*

When we start planning for our life and setting goals, we can easily become distracted by the "proverbial mile" in front of us. That mile can sometimes be our biggest opponent because the enormity of the work needed to achieve our dream can feel overwhelming. When we focus on the mile, we can quickly lose sight of the step. **When we lose sight of the step, we don't move. And when we don't move, our dreams, our desires, and potentially our destiny go unfulfilled.**

I have found myself stuck by the proverbial mile several times… overwhelmed by the big picture rather than focused on today's step. However, we have to look at the mile in order to know the step! If we never looked at it, we would never know what it takes to get where we want to go. But the problem is not in looking at the mile, it's *focusing* on it that can mess with us. When we are constantly evaluating and re-evaluating how close we are to finishing that mile, it can feel impossible. That's why before we start digging into setting goals, we need to train ourselves to think and act differently, focusing on one step at a time.

The mile (a.k.a. our ferocious enemy) is not as big and bad as he may seem. However, he'll creep up and have you stuck before you realize what's happening. In fact, the mile's job is to trick us into believing we can't accomplish the thing we desire; therefore, rendering us stagnant. He's a liar!

My wife and I were recently watching one of our favorite shows, *NCIS*—don't judge—and one of the main characters, Ducky, made this statement:

"When you are overwhelmed, do something you know you can accomplish and suddenly you won't be quite so overwhelmed."

I love this statement, especially for those moments where we are paralyzed by the overwhelming number of tasks we believe it will take to accomplish our goals; when we simply can't move or can't decide how to move. The reason we get stuck here is because we're looking at the wrong thing. **We're looking at everything we need to accomplish instead of looking at the one thing we can accomplish.**

I can get overwhelmed even after I've made a ton of progress. The great news is that *the biggest setbacks can be overcome by shifting your focus back to the smallest step.* This kind of refocusing is not a one-time occurrence. The mile will tempt you again and again, and that's OK.

When you're overwhelmed, stop and think about one small thing you *can* do now. Then make that your only goal. Look at it in the way that most of us look at buying a house or a car. Though the large item's sticker price is far out of reach, we focus our budget based on what the monthly payment will be. That's how you should tackle your mile. You know it's there, you understand it, but you are focusing on the monthly payment, so to speak, instead of focusing on paying off the entire loan.

When I was younger I was very athletic. I played basketball, ran track, and watched what I ate. Even after college I kept a pretty steady fitness regimen. Then I married my beautiful wife and started trading some of my gym time for hanging out on the couch with her. While that's a noble thing, unfortunately, my nobility packed on an extra 15 pounds. It shocked me a bit when I woke up one morning, looked in the mirror, and realized I wasn't so slim! I quickly kicked into gear and started getting up early and working out hard. I was young and it wasn't too long until I was back in shape. Fast-forward a few years to my wife's pregnancy. I tried so hard to maintain eating well, but it didn't last. *I needed to be sympathetic to my wife and help her eat all of that junk food our baby needed to grow.* Needless to say, I gained some extra weight.

After a year I still had that extra weight. I spent a year and a half not eating right and not working out because "I just didn't have the time, and it was too big of a commitment." I kept telling myself I didn't want to start working out unless I could "do it right." I figured if I worked out hard and ate a bit better, I could lose the extra pounds in three months. But then I kept trying to psych myself up for three months of sacrifice, and it just wasn't happening. While reflecting on that impending challenge ahead, I stayed on the couch eating pizza. I needed as much rest and food as I could get, because "when" I committed, it was going to be *tough!* I kept telling myself: "Only three months of sacrifice, *then* I can just maintain." Even though I hadn't maintained the last two times I had tested this same theory, I was sure this time would be different. Why I thought so, I don't know. Perhaps I was out to prove Einstein's definition of insanity: doing the same thing over and over and expecting different results.

Three months of sacrifice was my focus, *my proverbial mile*, when it should have been *my step*, simply ten minutes a day. Ten minutes doesn't sound that bad, but it doesn't sound that impactful either. Let me challenge your thinking when it comes to small steps.

Ten minutes a day will give you 10 times the results of zero minutes.

Compound that *10 times* over 30 days and you are 10 to the 30th power closer to your goal. That sounds pretty incredible when you think about it!

We just took that daunting mile and broke it into one small first step that has significantly more impact than it seemed to at the beginning. It definitely has more impact than doing nothing. And nothing is what most people will do when they focus on the mile instead of the step. Don't do nothing! Nothing breeds *nothing*. So, only do nothing if you want nothing.

What big challenge has been holding you back from moving forward in your work, marriage, dreams, or another area of your life? What step can you take today to get closer to where you want to be tomorrow? Let's break it down. Let's look at the impossible and figure out what's possible right now.

Remember: The goal is *consistent, incremental progress*. That's it. Just focus on the immediate road in front of you for now. Quit pondering the journey to the top of the mountain and just get to base camp!

Study Guide: *The Mile*

(Fill in the blanks or answer the questions from this lesson.)

When we start planning for our life and setting goals, we can easily become distracted by the "_____" in front of us.

When we focus on the mile, we can quickly lose sight of the step. When we lose sight of the step, we don't move. And when we don't move, our dreams, our desires, and potentially our destiny go _____.

We're looking at _____ we need to accomplish instead of looking at the _____ thing we can accomplish.

The great news is that the biggest setbacks can be overcome by shifting your focus back to the smallest _____.

When you're _____, stop and think about one small thing you can do now. Then make that your only goal.

What big challenge has been holding you back from moving forward in your work, marriage, dreams, or another area of your life?

_____

_____.

What step can you take today to get closer to where you want to be tomorrow?

_____

_____.

Notes: *The Mile*

Lesson 3: *Challenges in the Mile*

Imagine if our miles, dreams, or goals were like an Oklahoma mile instead of a Colorado mile!

I went to college in Tulsa, Oklahoma, and can remember the drive from my home in Arkansas to the campus. One of the most interesting things about that drive was how flat it was. You could literally see for miles. In fact, I can remember being almost *an hour* outside of the city and still being able to see three high-rise office buildings that marked my destination.

Many might go so far as to categorize this long, flat drive as *boring*… not me though, because I could go *fast*! There was absolutely nothing in my way and I could easily see a police officer from miles away. Maybe that's why I never seemed to see any officers. With nowhere to hide, they knew they could never catch anyone speeding!

If only our personal miles were like those Oklahoma miles. Unfortunately, they tend to be more like the notably contrasting Colorado miles. If you've ever snow skied in this part of the country you know exactly what I'm talking about—long, winding mountain roads… covered in snow. These roads are narrow, marked with danger on either side. You have to go slow. In fact, a mountain mile may take four times as long as an Oklahoma mile.

Our personal miles are typically more like this: You look down the road ahead and can't see the next turn. For example, you might think, "Maybe my boss will see my hard work and promote me." But there are no guarantees on that. The reality of life makes it difficult to go fast at times. Children still have to be cared for, bills have to be paid, and we will always feel pulled in multiple directions. And on top of that, we can't predict what's around the bend. You feel like you're risking everything with each turn, wondering the whole time if you should turn back. This is what we face when we look at our miles.

Two forces that create difficulties in our miles are **bad beliefs** and **past experiences**. These two roadblocks can place a negative filter on our miles. We see all of the reasons why "we can't," based on what we believe about ourselves or an experience we had, instead of seeing what is possible. These are real forces we fight against, but we have the ability to change our perspective with the *principle of progress*.

When I first started to write my book *Step*, the comments from well-meaning English teachers were all too vivid in my memory. They swam around in my head, as I thought, "I'm not a natural writer." My past experiences had formed an incorrect belief that began to dissuade me from even starting the journey. And there were definitely times in the middle of my journey when these beliefs would tempt me not to push forward, because "on my own I wasn't capable of producing something truly exceptional."

And that's it right there.

These beliefs cause us to stop. BUT the way to get past those hurdles is by moving forward in the midst of the bad beliefs so you can prove a new, more accurate belief about yourself.

We debunk bad beliefs with incremental wins. This is the whole *Step* principle, which you can find more of in my book. But the point is this: Every time I wrote a chapter or a post that someone liked, and even loved, it started to prove my beliefs were not just bad, but *false*. At that point, I had a decision on where to place my focus: the old, bad beliefs or my newfound *ability*. I chose the latter.

As for past experiences, they are in the past and that's where everything, except the lesson learned, will stay.

If you've been allowing the filter of bad beliefs and past experiences to stop you, try switching to a different filter. If you need more help, refer to my resources on Belief.

Whatever your mile, **there will be mountains** and mountains tend to be the most intimidating part of our miles. Mountains in our miles can take all types of shapes and forms. I have a good friend from South Africa who has lived in the United States for years now, and just recently took his test to become a citizen. That test was critical to protecting his ability to stay with his family, and it wasn't an easy one. He had to memorize 100 questions on American history and take a verbal test, given by an interviewer. And this intimidating interview was just a drop in the bucket compared to the mountain of paperwork and scrutiny he had to go through just to get the chance to interview.

For some, a mountain may take the form of a disability, a disease, or another type of medical condition. It could be the need for a certain amount of experience, the courage to make a pitch, or some form of news that seemingly doesn't allow you to move forward.

As you begin to approach the mountains in your mile or if you are already in the middle of it, here are a couple of things you can do in order to make your climb more successful:

1. Research the Best Path: What's the best path up the mountain? Is there a trail that's already been forged? Almost every mountain has already been climbed. And if it hasn't, there are usually similar mountains that have. One of the smartest things we can do when standing at the base of a mountain we're considering climbing is to research the best path up that mountain.

Honestly, I've struggled with this. My go-to seems to be "act now, ask later." And more often than not, I have found myself wasting time or dealing with undesirable consequences that could have been avoided if I had researched the experiences of the veterans before me.

So, research, research, research! Take the time to plan the *best* path up your mountain. You'll save yourself time and heartache, not to mention the fact that you'll be better prepared for what awaits you on the climb. And when you are prepared for the climb, your chances of reaching the top are much greater.

2. Prepare to Climb: Once you've researched your path and understand the demands of the mountain, you have to prepare for the climb. Preparation is both mental and physical. If you were to decide to climb Mt. Everest you wouldn't just show up and start climbing. You would prepare. You would buy special equipment, do practice climbs on smaller mountains, and exercise in order to increase your stamina. We have to do the same type of thing when it comes to the mountains in our miles. Every mountain is unique and preparation can look different for each climb, but typically the best way to know how to prepare is by finding out how past climbers prepared. How did the veterans before you prepare for the climb, or more importantly how did they *wish* they had prepared? Take the time to make a list of things you should do to prepare for the climb and start checking them off, one by one.

3. Remember the Descent: Every mountain has a descent or a point at which the climb has created momentum. There is a reason we're climbing and at the top of the mountain we can typically see the end of our mile. We can see our future in plain sight. *As we see the end of our mile in plain sight, we run with an ease that can only be created by the climb.* Like a rollercoaster at the top of its ascent, we are poised for the best part of this journey, the descent from the climb...you'll feel like you are flying!

So, when you are in the middle of your climb, remember what happens on the other side. You get to run faster than you ever thought possible toward the *end of your mile.* **The climb creates the momentum for a strong finish.** We know there will be mountains in our miles and we might even know what they are before we start. **However, it's the way we approach the mountains in our mile that will determine whether or not we see the top and experience the descent.**

Do the preliminary research to assess the mountains you will face as you accomplish your goals. How will you overcome those mountains? What is your route or strategy to get to the top? What preparation is critical? People talk about the mountains they scale for the rest of their lives. **Your mountains will define you. Be prepared to climb them.**

Study Guide: *Challenges in the Mile*

(Fill in the blanks or answer the questions from this lesson.)

Beliefs
We debunk bad beliefs with _____ wins.

What beliefs about yourself have been holding you back from achieving your goals?
_____
_____.

What's one thing you could do today that would start to prove your bad beliefs wrong?
_____

Past Experiences
As for past experiences, they are in the past and that's where everything except for the _____ will stay.

What past experiences have been holding you back from achieving your goals?
_____
_____.

What lessons could you learn and apply from your past experiences?
_____
_____.

Whatever your mile, there will be _____.

What are the mountains that you can see or are currently trying to climb in your mile?

_____

_____

Steps to Successfully Climbing the Mountain

1. **Research the Best Paths:** What are the different paths for successfully climbing the mountain in front of you? Research and write them down.

   _____

   _____

   _____

2. **Prepare to Climb:** What should be done to prepare for the climb?

   _____

   _____.

3. **Remember the Descent:** What will momentum feel like on the other side of the mountain?

   _____

   _____.

Notes: *Challenges in the Mile*

Lesson 4: *Discouragement of Distance*

What do a road trip and your mile have in common?

The answer: distance.

I've done quite a few road trips over the course of my life. Although I've never gone coast to coast, I have traveled from Dallas to New York and Dallas to California and back. And I have to admit, I'm not the biggest road trip fan in the world. Don't get me wrong, I have a blast, but not because of the driving!

My favorite part of the road trip is always the pit stops we make along the way. That, and reaching the destination, of course. But pit stops are the best! You get to stretch your legs and eat a ton of greasy food from a gas station or hole-in-the-wall café. And in my opinion, if you haven't eaten in one of those places where you find yourself wondering what exactly is happening in the kitchen and if the health department had visited lately… well, you haven't really lived!

Now, there are two types of people on road trips. The ones who love to take long pit stops and those who want to arrive at the destination as fast as possible and take the shortest pit stops imaginable. Either way, whether we like it or not, we need pit stops on long journeys to refuel and regain our bearings. The miles that make up the distance between who we are and who we want to be are exactly the same. They are typically long. Some feel like a cross-country road trip while others may feel like an intrastate drive. However, significant goals will have significant distance attached to them.

We should approach our goals and the miles that lay between like a long road trip. We should allow margin for pit stops. *And those breaks along the way to your goal should not be looked at as hassles that prevent us from moving forward*. Rather, they should be treated just like stopping for gas or food… They are critical. **Pit stops are our time to refuel, rest, and recalibrate for the trek ahead.**

Refueling. Depending on the vehicle you drive, you'll have to refuel every several hundred miles. Your vehicle literally will stop in the middle of the road if you don't. However, we often don't think about ourselves the same way, but we are just like cars in this sense. Eating is one of our ways to refuel. But when it comes to goals, refueling can look like a lot of things depending on the mile you're on.

What is the *fuel* to your goal?

Often times it's taking the time to look up from our steps and see the progress we've made. I've often used the phrase, "Progress is our fuel to keep going," and that definitely applies here. **Whatever your method of refueling may be, do it and do it often!** Don't fall into the trap of thinking that you can run on empty forever. If you do, you might find yourself burned out or giving up on your goal completely.

Rest. It is a necessary part of a successful journey. Rest is different than refueling. Refueling is about doing something to put energy back in. Rest is simply about repairing. We need rest. Even the best and most physically fit athletes have days of rest from working out in order to let their bodies heal and recover from the hard work they've been doing.

Rest heals. When we are exhausted, our decisions aren't as well thought out, our emotions aren't as checked, and we are actually not as productive. A day off is often the best way to keep going! Again rest will be different for each person and the journey you are on, but it's important to give yourself a break. And if you aren't one who is very good at resting… it might be a good time for you to find a friend who is and ask their advice.

Rest is important. **The break doesn't have to be long, it just needs to be consistent and allow you to take a deep breath.** Plan for a break!

Recalibrate. After you have refueled and rested on your pit stop, you'll find it's time to get back on the road. However, before you pull out of the gas station, you'll want to take a look at the map and recalibrate your expectations and goals for the next leg of the trip. Recalibrating is something many of us do every morning to a small degree.

Before I jump into some form of work activity every morning, I pull out a notepad and start thinking about what needs to be accomplished that day. I think about my weekly and monthly goals that ultimately ladder up to my life goals. Then I plan my day accordingly.

Think about this time like an app on your phone, "recalculating the fastest route" to your destination. Things change and they change quickly. **When we don't take the time to recalibrate, we might be forcing ourselves to take the longer path or the harder path.** Ask yourself, *What did I learn from the last leg of the trip that should inform the next?* This could be related to daily actions, a change in our ultimate destination, or simply a better way of doing what we've been doing all along.

Your plan to recalibrate should be mapped and tweaked as you travel these long stretches. Miles are long and with length come the temptations to give up or begin believing the things you want are impossible.

Our miles were not meant to be traveled all at once, so take pit stops on a regular basis. Plan them by placing time on your calendar or aligning with milestones. (We'll talk about milestones in Lesson 11.) Stay attuned to the demands this journey is requiring of you and incorporate your refueling, rest, and recalibration accordingly.

Study Guide: *Discouragement of Distance*

(Fill in the blanks or answer the questions from this lesson.)

Pit stops are our time to _____, _____, and _____ for the trek ahead.

_____ is our fuel to keep going.

What have you found to be your best way to refuel? (e.g., exercise, celebration, time with friends)

_____

Rest is simply about _____.

What activities leave you feeling the most rested?

_____

_____

When we don't take the time to _____, we might be forcing ourselves to take the longer path or the harder path.

When recalibrating, ask yourself, what did I learn from the last leg of the trip that should inform the next?

_____

_____

Notes: *Discouragement of Distance*

Lesson 5: *Breaking Down the Mile (Overview)*

Our vision is big and so are the proverbial miles that come with it!

As we look down our mile, we see all types of obstacles such as bad beliefs and past experiences. We see the mountains that sit in the middle of our mile and the corners that hold the "unknowns" that are lurking in the dark, waiting to stop us from finishing. However, we've decided to move forward in the midst of all these obstacles, because we know that it's worth it!

So what now?

Let's break the mile down. **Let's look at the impossible and figure out what's possible.** But before we start down this path, I want to be clear on what this exercise is—and what it isn't. It's not a way of cataloging every single step necessary. You can't take something as intricate as, say, starting a business and capture every moving detail in a single line of steps. But you *can* look at something huge and break it down to the first set of steps you need to get started.

The goal is *consistent incremental progress*.

That's it. Just focus on the immediate road in front of you for now. As you progress, you can use this principle any time you're stuck. Something like starting a business will have several monumental miles lurking within it, some more complicated than others. Just break them down, so you can keep going. The inverse is true for more simplistic goals, like eating healthy or exercising. You can break the whole mile into one linear set of steps—or even just one step on repeat: *Write every day. Eat one healthy meal a day. Work out for 15 minutes each day.*

Simple or complex, you still need to break the thing down. This part is fun, because you can use a formula. Yes, you can actually plug that scary, overwhelming thing into a formula that will spit out the answers for you. My favorite formula for this exercise comes from the computer science world and uses one of the most common logic expressions: the *if–then* statement. Don't worry if you're not computer savvy, this will be painless. In fact, you might understand programming more than you thought.

Here's how it works:

If [insert the condition], then [insert the command or action].

Here's an example:
If I want to own a house ("own a house" being the condition), **then I need to buy a house** ("buy the house" being the command or action).

Pretty basic, right? It's logical and that's why they call it a logic—or logical—expression. Let's take this same example and expand it. If I want to own a house, then I need to buy a house. If I need to buy a house, then I need to save money for a down payment. If I need to save money for a down payment, then I need to lower my monthly expenses. If I need to find ways to lower my monthly expenses, then I need to eat out less, or then I need to be more efficient with my electricity consumption, or then I need to consider renting my current place on Airbnb.

Most of us have probably gone through this thought process without being so deliberate. In fact, we do it every day. We are constantly assessing what's needed to accomplish the task in front of us, then we do those things. *It's called being logical.* However, if you can get a better understanding of how you can jump-start the logical side of your brain when you're having a hard time… well, that's a nice tool to have!

In the example above, we found three very attainable steps to take toward saving money to buy a house. You might be thinking, "This is all pretty obvious," and it is. **The trick is to apply this logic to the goals we've had a hard time breaking down.** When we apply this formula to our miles and the challenges that lay within our miles, we find that climbing the mountains of past experiences or bad beliefs are not quite so intimidating.

Start thinking about your miles today as a series of inches, feet, or yards that build upon each other to reach your ultimate destination. This will immediately start to demystify the "how" to defeating your mile. Think through one area and practice using the *if–then* statements to create a clear path in front of you.

Remember, you will want to use logic to break down your steps while you think outside of the box to map out creative ways to achieve your goal!

Study Guide: *Breaking Down the Mile (Overview)*

(Fill in the blanks or answer the questions from this lesson.)

Let's look at the _____ and figure out what's _____.

But you *can* look at something huge and break it down to the _____ you need to get started.

The goal is _____ incremental progress.

My favorite formula for this exercise comes from the computer science world and uses one of the most common logic expressions: the _____ statement.

Here's how it works:

If _____ [insert condition/goal/dream],

then _____ [insert command/or necessary action/step].

Example

    If I want to own a house,
    then I need to buy a house.

Pretty basic, right? It's logical and that's why they call it a logic or logical expression. Let's keep going.

If I want to own a house,
then I need to buy a house.

If I need to buy a house,
then I need to find a house to buy.

If I need to find a house to buy,
then I should look for a house.

If I should look for a house,
then I should call a Realtor.
Or
then I should drive around looking for "for sale" signs.
Or
then I should download a real estate app.

Notes: *Breaking Down the Mile (Overview)*

Lesson 6: *Breaking Down the Mile (Defining It)*

When my wife and I were first married, we barely earned enough money to cover our monthly expenses. However, we had five financial goals that we were committed to, and we wanted to continue working toward them even though our situation wasn't the greatest.

Our five goals were:

1. Paying off debt.

2. A Future Child savings account, which meant saving a $10,000 safety net for when we had our first child.

3. An Investment account, which meant accumulating funds for investment opportunities, such as buying a rental house.

4. A Fun account, which is exactly what it sounds like… we wanted to save money for fun things like vacations, concerts, etc.

5. A Giving account. We wanted to save money so we could continually provide money to needs we saw in our community.

At the time, every one of these items seemed impossible. We had absolutely no room in our budget. But we believed strongly in the principle of *Step*, and we were determined to find a way to start working toward the things that we wanted in our future.

My original thought was to put a percentage of our income toward each of these categories so that once we were making more money, the amounts being deposited in each of these goal accounts would increase. We started very small and decided that, no matter what, we would put 1% of our income toward these things each month. That equated to roughly $5 in each account at the time.

Here is what the *if–then* statement for this scenario looked like:

If I want to pay off debt, save for my kids, have money to invest, spend money for fun, and give money when needs arise, then I need to start putting money toward each of these goals. If I need to start putting money toward each of these goals, then I need to determine an amount to put toward these goals each time I receive money. If I need to determine an amount to put toward these goals each time I receive money, then I need to find a percentage that I can feel comfortable with saving when I receive money *and* then I need to determine what to do when I receive money I wasn't expecting.

One of the most critical things to do when we're breaking down our miles is to clearly define the mile first. It seems pretty basic, but a well-defined goal is often overlooked.

"A problem well stated is a problem half solved."
—Charles Kettering

Amy and I broke our goal down and that's what mattered at the time. However, we could have done a better job of defining our mile. Creating that clear definition of your mile starts by creating your *if* statement. The *if* statement is the "problem well stated."

You can create a great *if* statement by asking some questions. Effective *if* questions can be created by asking these three questions:

1. What do I want?

2. When do I want it?

3. Can I quantify it?

Here's an example of what this could look like with a real goal:

What? I want to pay off my mortgage.
When? In five years and
The **quantity** would be how much I owe.

Let's say it's $150,000. Now, we put this all together to form our *if* statement:

If I want to pay off my mortgage of $150,000 in five years…

That's our *if* statement clearly defined. Once we've created a clear and concise *if* statement, we can start to break it down, and we're going to do that in a following lesson.

Don't worry if your statement feels impossible. It probably will be at this point and that's okay! For most people the idea of paying off an additional $150k in five years might seem crazy, but once we apply the entire formula, you'll find it's not so far-fetched.

The reason I took an entire lesson to define our *if* statements thoroughly is because it gets skipped over way too often. This is your day to specify what you want with clarity. So, take some time today or in the next couple of days to spell out your *if* statements clearly.

Study Guide: *Breaking Down the Mile (Defining It)*

(Fill in the blanks or answer the questions from this lesson.)

Let's look at the _____ and figure out what's _____.

You *can* look at something huge and break it down to the _____ you need to get started.

Start by creating your *if* statement. Be as clear and detailed as possible. I recommend using three questions:

1. What do I want?
2. When do I want it?
3. Can I quantify it?

For example:
   What? I want to pay off my mortgage.
   When? In five years and
   The **quantity** is the amount I owe ($150,000).

If statement: If I want to pay off my mortgage ($150k) in five years…

Exercise

Use what, when, and quantity to create your first *if* statement.

What: _____

When: _____

Quantify: _____

If Statement (Your Mile):

_____

Notes: *Breaking Down the Mile (Defining It)*

Lesson 7: *Breaking Down the Mile (Creating Steps)*

As we've been breaking down the mile, we talked last about making sure the mile is well defined. When we use our *if–then* statement and have a well-defined *if* statement, we are on our way to creating great next steps! But what exactly are those next steps?

In a previous example, we set our *if* statement to: If I want to pay off my mortgage of $150,000 in five years… We have a clear goal and we know where we want to end up, but what do we do next? Where do we start? Is there a right or wrong way to start?

In order to figure out where to start, we must break our miles (a.k.a. goals) down into *steps*. **Steps are the bite-size morsels of action that we can take no matter what our life looks like**. It's how we keep moving in the midst of everyday life.

Now let's continue with the example of paying off our mortgage in five years. My guess is that for most of us this probably seems a bit impossible. That's perfect, because we're going to break this mile down into something that is believable.

If I want to pay off my mortgage of $150k in five years, then I need to pay off $30k per year. If I need to pay off $30k per year, then I need to pay off $2,500 per month. If I need to pay off $2,500 per month, then I need to pay off $625 per week. If I need to pay off $625 per week, then I need to pay off $125 per day (assuming a five-day workweek). If I need to pay off $125 per day (assuming a five-day workweek), then I need to make an extra $16 per hour (assuming eight hours per day, five days per week).

Let's stop for a second. It's important to walk through the entire process and not shortchange it before you've broken it down to the ridiculous. Some may say, "Chris, I can break it down all day long, but an extra $150k over five years just isn't possible no matter how you look at it." That's the problem, you're not allowing yourself to look at the situation from a different perspective. You're still focusing on the mile, and as long as you focus on the *mile* you'll never see the *step*. Okay, let's keep going.

What would you need to do in order to make an extra $16 each hour (assuming a 40-hour workweek) to pay off your mortgage?
… Then I should look for jobs that pay $16 more per hour.
… Then I should gain the skills to get the job that makes $16 more per hour.
or
… Then I need to find a way to sell five things five days a week for $25 each.
… Then I need to find something I can sell and make $25 on.

or

… Then I need to make an extra $5 per hour and cut monthly expenses by $1,700.

… Then I need to ask my boss about a plan to make $5 more per hour and cut cable, eating out budget, etc.

Hopefully you're seeing the pattern by now. **Open your mind to what you can do, not what you can't do.** You can't pay off $150k in five years if you don't know where to start. It may start by using Netflix instead of cable. That's a step toward the goal. Will that alone get you to your goal? No, but it's a step in the right direction. *More importantly, it's not a step in the wrong direction.*

When you put this formula in place you will find steps that you can start to take immediately. The challenge is to take them no matter how small or insignificant they may seem. Start breaking down your mile now!

Here are a few quick tips for breaking down your miles:

1. Write down every step. It may feel a bit unnecessary, but I need you to trust the process. Write down every single step you can think of when breaking down your mile. It doesn't matter how obvious that step may be or how unattainable it may seem. No matter how small, obvious, or silly the step may seem, you'll have to take it if you want to finish the mile. Write it down.

2. Write down every possible way to do a step. In our example, I found three different paths to paying off the house in five years. I want you to find every possible path, even if it's not a path you want to go down or believe you can. Understanding your options is critical to making a clear decision to step. Also, sometimes it's a combination of several options that creates your ultimate path.

3. Do not worry about *believing* it. As you go through this process, and especially as you start breaking down your mile, you will write down things you don't believe you can accomplish. **Look past your belief for a moment and keep writing.** Sometimes it may even help to get a friend to break down your mile with you or someone who has walked the path before.

If you don't follow the process because you don't believe you can do one *step* in it, you're selling yourself short and will most likely never achieve your goal. What's the harm in trusting me?

Get a little ridiculous and start breaking your *mile* into *steps* today!

Study Guide: *Breaking Down the Mile (Creating Steps)*

Let's review using the same *if* statement example:

If I want to pay off my mortgage ($150k) in five years,
Then I need to pay off $30k per year.

If I need to pay off $30k per year,
Then I need to pay off $2,500 per month.

If I need to pay off $2,500 per month,
Then I need to pay off $625 per week.

If I need to pay off $625 per week,
Then I need to pay off $125 per day, assuming five-day workweek.

If I need to pay off $125 per day, assuming five-day workweek,
Then I need to make an extra $16 per hour, assuming eight hours per day, five days per week.

Let's stop for a second. It's important to walk through the entire process and not shortchange it before you've broken it down to the ridiculous. Some people may say, "Chris, I can break it down all day long, but an extra $150k over five years just isn't possible no matter how you look at it." That is the problem... you're not allowing yourself to look at the situation in a different light. You're still focusing on the mile, and as long as you focus on the mile, you'll never see the step.

Okay. Let's keep going. What would you need to do in order to make an extra $16 each hour (assuming a 40-hour workweek) to pay off your mortgage?

Then I should look for jobs that pay $16 more per hour…
Then I should gain the skills to get the job that makes $16 more per hour…
or
Then I need to find a way to sell 5 things 5 days a week for $25…
Then I need to find something I can sell and make $25 on…
or
Then I need to make an extra $5 per hour and cut monthly expenses by $1,700…
Then I need to ask my boss about a plan to make $5 more per hour and cut cable, eating out budget, etc.

Hopefully you're seeing the pattern by now. Open your mind to what you can do, not what you can't do. You can't pay off $150k in five years if you don't know where to start.

It may start by using Netflix instead of cable. That's a step toward the goal.

Will that alone get you to your goal? No, but it's a step in the right direction.

More importantly, it's not a step in the wrong direction. When you put this formula into place, you will find steps that you can start to take. The challenge is to take them no matter how small or insignificant they may seem. Let's start breaking down your mile now!

Exercise

Insert your *if* statement from the last lesson in the starting *If* blank below and start breaking down your mile. Additional statements can be written in the worksheet at the end of this workbook.

If _____

Then _____

If _____

Then _____

If _____

Then _____

If _____

Then _____

If _____

Then _____

If _____

Then _____

If _____

Then _____ **= Your Step**

Notes: *Breaking Down the Mile (Creating Steps)*

Use the notes section to continue breaking down your mile into steps if needed.

Lesson 8: *Celebrating Milestones*

Every *step* is worth celebrating!

Every time we make a push, be it big or small, toward the desired end, we are taking control of our life.

I remember the first time I heard someone say, "We should celebrate small victories." It was my college professor Dr. Lewandowski. He had been a successful businessman in the medical field before selling his company and deciding to teach "Creativity in Business." This class was my favorite business class because he broke the norm for traditional teaching methods. For instance, once he had us take a nap in class. Seriously! As he was wrapping up a lecture, he told us to bring a pillow and a blanket to the next class, then he had us take a nap during that next class!

There was a point to the odd assignment, of course, and it was learning the importance of rest. As we rested, he took us through an exercise showing us how to get in a quiet place in order to focus. He broke the norm. Dr. Lew would often tell us the story of how in his previous company he created a *culture* of celebrating small wins. One of the ways he did this was with a putting green. He had a makeshift putting green in the office and every time the team would close a deal, they'd play a game or do something else fun. They didn't take eight hours to celebrate, but they broke away for a few minutes to recognize the progress they had made toward their overall goal.

I want to talk about the importance of breaking down our mile into notable milestones worthy of celebrating! When we break our *miles* into *steps*, we instinctively begin to focus on those steps and that's exactly what we should do. In our mile there are inches, feet, yards, and so on. **We have to travel every single one of those inches, feet, or yards to get where we want to go.**

A milestone is a predefined point along the path where you look up and glance back at how far you've come, and celebrate it. This means, once we've plotted the steps we need to take, we should plot the milestones as well. When we combine these together we can see tangible, significant progress toward our goal.

Look back at the *if–then* statements you created when breaking down your mile and identify the milestones. For example: As I was writing *Step*, the completion of each chapter was one of my milestones.

Why is the celebration of milestones so important? *If we only focus on taking steps and never feel truly accomplished until we reach the end of our goal, there is a high probability that we will find ourselves discouraged or just living for the end, instead of enjoying the journey.* And since most of our life is some type of journey, we need to learn to enjoy it. **Though they may seem small, milestones are significant and should be celebrated!**

In my book *Step,* I talk about how *perspective can be the antidote to giving up on our goals.* One of the ways we can maintain a positive perspective through the mile is by focusing on the reason(s) we are stepping—the "why" at the end of our mile. Apply this same concept to a milestone. Here's a question you can ask yourself if you're having trouble finding the milestones in your mile:

If I _____, I will have proven to myself and the world that I'm on my way to accomplishing _____.

Some examples could be:
If I lose five pounds, I will have proven to myself and the world that I'm on my way to accomplishing my goal of losing 100 pounds.
If I pay off $1,000 of my debt, I will have proven to myself and the world that I'm on my way to paying off all of my debt.
If I get my first customer, I will have proven to myself and the world that I'm on my way to running my own successful business.

Once you've identified your milestones, start working to reach them. Once you reach them, celebrate! Take a deep breath and enjoy the taste of success.

Our life and our goals are a journey. **We must celebrate the milestones if we want to enjoy the journey.**

Study Guide: *Celebrating Milestones*

(Fill in the blanks or answer the questions from this lesson.)

Every step is worth _____.

A _____ is a predefined point along the path where you look up and glance back at how far you've come, and celebrate it.

Once we've plotted the steps we need to take, we should _____ the milestones as well.

We must celebrate the milestones if we want to enjoy the _____ .

Exercise

Use the following question to help create a milestone:

If I _____ (e.g., lose five pounds), I will have proven to myself and the world that I'm on my way to accomplishing _____ (losing 100 pounds).

If I _____ (e.g., lose five pounds), I will have proven to myself and the world that I'm on my way to accomplishing _____ (losing 100 pounds).

List at least three milestones in your mile and how you plan to celebrate:

_____ (milestone) = _____ (celebration)

_____ (milestone) = _____ (celebration)

_____ (milestone) = _____ (celebration)

_____ (milestone) = _____ (celebration)

Notes: *Celebrating Milestones*

Lesson 9: *Complex Miles*

My friend climbed Pikes Peak several years ago. This massive mountain in the Colorado Rockies is known for being a difficult climb and for its towering altitude. The beginning is a pretty standard mountain climb with trees, vegetation, and majestic views. However, at 11,500 feet in elevation the tree line fades away as the environment won't support tree life anymore. Breathing becomes substantially more difficult as oxygen decreases. As you begin to approach the summit, you enter into what people call the 16 Golden Stairs. When an amateur hiker approaches this section, it can be quite exciting. After all, every time you reach the top of one staircase you feel like you are almost there. But the problem with these stairs is that they are misleading. What an inexperienced hiker takes at face value—16 golden stairs—a pro understands differently. A "stair" refers to a *set* of switchbacks. One left-hand switchback and one right-hand switchback combined make for one "stair." And if you count them it's more difficult. With a hike like this so far above the tree line, a hiker (especially one not used to the altitude) has to make a calculated plan for catching his/her breath and for making it through the next set of switchbacks. In the end, the summit is breathtaking. But the rigorous process of getting there takes many calculated steps, and sometimes the steps you take end up being more difficult and take longer than you expected.

The mistake that is often made for the amateur hiking Pikes Peak in the 16 Golden Stairs scenario is that he or she makes a plan for how they are going to accomplish the 16 stairs at the beginning, but when they are hit with 32+ switchbacks, an unknown finish line, and low oxygen, they aren't quite ready for it! One of the mistakes we can make as we are planning our mile is to attempt to plan out every single step it'll take us to reach the end, without making allowances for some adjustments along the way that might change how we need to execute our future steps.

The point of breaking down your mile is to find the *next* step, not *every* step.

Reaching your ultimate goal is often the result of accomplishing a *series of moving targets* that require adjustment and refocus on a constant basis. We should be *continually* breaking down our miles, not doing it one time and thinking we are good for a lifetime. Steps are simple, but miles tend to be complex. In fact, the reason we need that simplicity is because of the complexity of the mile.

For example: losing weight. Although this isn't an easy goal, the steps are fairly well documented and repeatable: exercise, food planning, accountability, etc. For most people a strict commitment to doing these well-researched tasks over a period of time will lead to weight loss. This isn't necessarily considered a complex mile, although it may be a difficult one.

On the other hand, what if your mile is starting a profitable business? Off the top of my head you need to determine a product, find a market, figure out how to appeal to that market, create a website, start a legal entity, get funding, get customers, and the list goes on and on and on. Starting a business isn't quite as cut and dry as losing weight.

You can apply the step principles to a business, but you'll have a more difficult time knowing every step before you start. **The point is to start, and find the most important step for today.** Regarding a business, it will usually start with what you are going to sell and who is going to buy it. In the more complex miles we often see the third and fourth steps by taking the first and second.

My hope in this lesson is to give you a bit of ease in understanding that breaking down your mile is not about plotting your entire course (that is overwhelming!), but to find the most important steps for *today*, then *do* them. **Tomorrow's steps will come on the heels of yesterday's steps** or by going through the process again. If you're the type of person that needs to know every step before you get started, you'll struggle with the more complex goals in life. There is uncertainty in every mile. There will be days where you feel like your step doesn't matter. There will be days when you can't seem to figure out what to do next. On those days, you will go back to the process of breaking down your mile into the *next* step, not *every* step.

Today, take some time to write down any area where you see you've struggled to take the first step due to fear of not knowing all the steps. Look at what that first step would be and *take it*.

Study Guide: *Complex Miles*

(Fill in the blanks or answer the questions from this lesson.)

One of the _____ we can make as we are planning our mile is to attempt to plan out _____ single step it'll take us to reach the end.

The point of breaking down your mile is to find the _____ step, not _____ step.

Reaching your ultimate goal is often the result of accomplishing a series of _____ targets that require adjustment and refocus on a constant basis.

We should be _____ breaking down our miles, not doing it one time and thinking we are good for a lifetime.

Steps are simple, but miles tend to be _____ . In fact, the reason we need that simplicity is because of the mile's complexity.

The point is to find the _____ for today, then do them.

Tomorrow's _____ will come on the heels of yesterday's steps or by going through the process again.

There will be days when you can't seem to figure out what to do next. And on those days you go back to the process of _____ your mile into the *next* _____ , not *every* step.

In what areas have you struggled to take the first step due to fear of not knowing all the steps?

_____

_____

Consider taking that first step today, knowing that it will reveal the next step.

Notes: *Complex Miles*

Lesson 10: *Commitment*

When we break down our miles, we need to understand the effort involved to achieve them. Let's continue with the example of paying off your house. Our *if* statement was:

If I want to pay off my mortgage of $150k in five years...

We then broke that down into several options that included different steps that could make that possible. One involved getting training to increase our pay. Another was based on finding a product to sell, and the third was a hybrid of both cutting expenses and finding a higher-paying job. Feel free to refer back to this example in Chapter 3 of *Step*, "Breaking Down the Proverbial Mile."

Each one of the steps required to accomplish the overarching goal of paying off a mortgage in five years demands a level of commitment. This is the same for any goal. If reaching your goal didn't require commitment above and beyond what you're currently doing, then you would already be on track to accomplishing it, and you wouldn't be here, reading this!

I always encourage people to put quantity and time on their goals, and I do that for a reason. If you don't have them, then you won't actually understand the level of commitment it will take to reach them. **Once you've figured out how long it will take to accomplish your goals and the commitment required, you have the power to "turn the dials."**

You may determine that paying off your home in five years is not something you're willing to commit to, but you might be willing to do it in ten. The fun thing about breaking down your miles is that you can go back through the exercise with ease by simply adjusting time and/or quantity. I run across people every day that have a big goal but couldn't tell you what it would actually take to achieve it. And since they can't tell you what it takes to achieve their goal, for them, the goal can seem somewhat intangible. And if it remains that way, then there's an excuse for not achieving it. I don't want you to have an excuse for not achieving your goals!

That's why understanding what it takes and assessing your willingness to make the commitment to go after it is so important.

When I decided to write *Step*, I knew it would possibly take several years at the pace I was running for the book to be published. However, knowing that up front gave me the information I needed to make a sober judgment as to whether or not I'd be willing to commit to that type of an endeavor. This is the fringe benefit of breaking down your miles into the "ridiculously small steps" that I harp on so much. **Not only do you figure out *what* you need to do today, but you also figure *how much* of it you need to do to get where you're going.**

So, look at your goal. Then look at the steps you've broken down to get there. Be realistic with yourself. Before you start, determine whether or not you're willing to commit to the time and effort it will take to achieve those goals.

Time and effort are two fundamental pieces to achieving anything of significance.

Don't start if you're not willing to put the time and effort in, or you'll only find yourself disillusioned and disappointed when you fail to hit your goals. Evaluate your goals and the time and effort each will require to pull off. Then ask yourself: *Am I willing to make that investment?*

Study Guide: *Commitment*

(Fill in the blanks or answer the questions from this lesson.)

I always encourage people to put _____ and _____ on their goals, and I do that for a reason. If you don't have them, then you won't actually understand the level of _____ (commitment) it will take to reach them.

Once you've figured out how long it will take to accomplish your goals and the commitment required, you have the power to "_____."

I don't want you to have an _____ for not achieving your goals. That's why understanding what it takes and assessing your willingness to make the _____ to go after it is so important.

Make a list of your goals (miles).

Goal: Write a book in two years.

Time/Effort: Two hours per week.

Commit: Yes or No

Goal: _____

Time/Effort: _____

Commit: Yes or No

If no, why?
_____

If yes, what will you have to adjust in your life to make room for the time and effort required?

_____

Notes: *Commitment*

Lesson 11: *People and Our Goals*

"A body of men, holding themselves accountable to nobody, ought not to be trusted by anybody."
—Thomas Paine, one of America's Founding Fathers

I'm a big believer in trusting yourself. But when it comes to accomplishing goals, I tend to side with Thomas Paine. **When we are accountable to ourselves, we are the only ones who can hold ourselves responsible.** And let's face it, we love us! So more often than not, we will go easy on ourselves. If we miss a time line or choose not to step and nobody else knows about it, what happens? It's kind of like the saying, "If a tree falls in the forest and nobody is around to hear it, does it make a sound?" Sure it does. But it can't be proven, since nobody is there to witness it. Our goals are very similar, and it's critical that we're not the only people that know about them.

Positive peer pressure is a real thing, and I believe it's a good thing. As a general rule, we are motivated by what other people think and say of us. When we know people are watching, we tend to work harder and follow through on our commitments. *Accountability plays a critical role in accomplishing goals.* Ask yourself these three questions:

1. Who knows about my goal?

2. Who knows my daily commitment to that goal?

3. Who will keep me accountable?

Find one or more people to fill the role of keeping you accountable to your goal. Give them permission to call you out and set a schedule for check-ins to report your progress.

Sometimes, when we think about goal setting, we think of ourselves as *individuals* accomplishing that goal, but maybe we were never meant to accomplish it on our own at all. Beyond needing people to hold us accountable to outcomes, we need people to help us in the *process* of achieving our goals.

This could come in the form of a mentor, coach, or consultant. Sometimes you need to add people to your team in order to complete your goals.

Have you ever thought about what it takes to climb a mountain? We can climb small mountains in our spare time and on our own. But it's more fun to do it with someone else. And the taller the mountain that you want to climb, the more important it becomes to take a team with you. Writing *Step* was a team effort. Sure, in the beginning it depended on me to take the ball down the field. But in order to meet my goal of writing a book people wanted to read, it required a developmental editor, a copy editor, and more.

Beyond finding people to be accountable to, you need to find people who can assist you on your journey. I've never accomplished anything significant on my own. There has always been someone or a group of people who have helped me. Sometimes these people were paid members of a team, but in many cases they were friends who went above and beyond to help a friend in the pursuit of his dreams.

When it comes to achieving your goals, you will need to find people who can keep you accountable and people who can assist you. Choosing to go after your goal alone is choosing to bet against yourself. Why would you ever choose to bet against yourself?

Take time today to identify your team and ask them to participate in making your goal a reality.

Study Guide: *People and Our Goals*
(Fill in the blanks or answer the questions from this lesson.)

Thomas Paine once said, *"A body of men, holding themselves accountable to _____, ought not to be trusted by _____."*

When we are accountable to _____, we are the only ones who can hold ourselves responsible. And let's face it, we love us. So more often than not, we will go easy on ourselves.

_____ plays a critical role in accomplishing goals.

Three Questions to Ask Yourself

1. Who knows about your goal?

_____

2. Who knows your daily commitment to that goal?

_____

3. Who will keep you accountable?

_____

Beyond finding people to be accountable to, you need to find people who can _____ you on your journey.

Choosing to go after your goal _____ is choosing to bet against yourself.

In the pursuit of your goals, who do you need to add to your team?

_____

_____

_____

Notes: *People and Our Goals*

Lesson 12: *Winning the Day*

Will we achieve our goals or not? That is the question!

We answer this question daily with the actions we choose to take or not take. When we wake up in the morning, our goals are sitting on the shelf wondering whether or not we will pick them up. Will we sleep in just a little bit longer and put off today what we can surely do tomorrow? Will we choose some form of momentary comfort instead of choosing to step toward our goals? These questions are answered every single day, and the cumulative response to those questions indicates whether or not achieving our goals will become a reality. **My whole philosophy and the goal of *Step* is to make it clear that any large goal can be broken down into bite-size or daily chunks that we believe we can accomplish.**

I did this with *Step*, and I'm still doing it today. I planned this lesson at 6:30 a.m. in Nashville, Tennessee, on a business trip. My day was jam-packed and the only way I could create my plan for this lesson was to work on it early, while I was fresh. I had a decision to make: I could stay up late in my hotel room and watch TV or go to bed early so I could get to a coffee shop and write before my 8:00 a.m. meeting. Thankfully, I made the right choice, and you have this lesson in your hands because of that decision.

When it comes to your goals, your day is your most important asset. How you plan it and how you use it determines your future. There is one thing you can and should do daily in order to stay on track with your goals: **Schedule your day before it starts.** Scheduling is quite possibly one of the most important determining factors in achieving one's goals. Show me a person who does this, and I'll show you a person who achieves what they set out to do. There are three things we should schedule:

1. We should schedule time to work on our goals.

2. We should schedule what we are going to do.

3. We should schedule tomorrow.

Schedule time to work on your goals before the day starts. When I went to bed in Nashville knowing exactly what my plan was for the next day, I didn't have to think about it when I woke up. And because I had planned for it, it was accomplished!

Not only did I know the time, but I knew the "what" as well. That's right, we have to schedule more than just the time. We also need to schedule *what* we will be doing. I knew when I woke up that morning that I was going to a coffee shop close to my meeting to write this exact lesson. Sometimes we might think the "what" is obvious.

For instance, "I'm going to work on my goal of writing a book." That's not specific enough. The less specific we are when scheduling the "what," the more likely we will waste time and become distracted by things that don't truly matter. This happens because **when making decisions in the moment, we tend to choose the path of least resistance instead of most importance**. Don't leave it to chance. It's so easy to waste valuable time trying to figure out what to do if you haven't already made that decision! If I would have walked into that coffee shop not knowing what I was going to work on, I would have most likely wasted a considerable amount of time trying to figure it out.

The last point is to *schedule the next time to work on your goal* and specifically what part of it you're going to work on. Before I left the coffee shop that morning, I scheduled my next time to work on my goal. Not only did I schedule the next time, but I scheduled the next *thing* I was going to do.

Scheduling this way leads to efficiency and also increases the likelihood of success. Not only that, but I've found that scheduling the time and the "what" leads to less stress in the pursuit of my goals. It leads to less stress because I'm not worrying about how, when, or what I'm going to do next. I've already taken the time to schedule the details of all of those things.

If you schedule your time to act, you will decrease your stress and increase your ability to win!

Schedule your time and your "what" today!

Study Guide: *Winning the Day*

(Fill in the blanks or answer the questions from this lesson.)

When it comes to your goals, your _____ is your most important asset.

_____ your day before it starts.

Scheduling is quite possibly one of the most _____ determining factors in achieving one's goals.

Three Things We Should Schedule

1. Schedule _____ to work on our goals.

2. Schedule _____ we're going to do.

3. Schedule _____.

When making decisions in the _____, we tend to choose the path of _____ resistance instead of most importance. So don't leave it to chance.

If you schedule your time to _____, you'll decrease your _____ and _____ your ability to win the day!

Notes: *Winning the Day*

Worksheet: *Breaking Down the Mile*

The following is an outline for how you can break down your mile. Use it as a guide to get started.

What: _____

When: _____

Quantify: _____

If Statement (Your Mile)

Exercise

Insert your *if* statement from Lesson 10 in the starting *If* blank below and start breaking down your mile.

If _____

Then _____

If _____

Then _____

If _____

Then _____

If _____

Then _____

If _____

Then _____

If _____

Then _____

If _____

Then _____

If _____

Then _____

If _____

Then _____

If _____

Then _____

If _____

Then _____

If _____

Then _____ **= Your Step**

If _____

Then _____ **= Your Step**

If _____

Then _____ **= Your Step**

About Chris Capehart

"My dad was a pastor and cheated on my mom. She committed suicide. He died of cancer. I defied the odds and so can you."

Chris' story is proof that though life rarely gives us what we hope for, we can still beat the odds and achieve a meaningful life. Every challenge presents a choice: a choice either to let circumstances define us or to do exactly the opposite. Chris has made it a point to do exactly the opposite by defining his own life and taking purposeful steps to overcome every challenge thrown his way. His fresh approach to overcoming the inevitable challenges life brings will inspire and motivate people from all walks of life to connect with their purpose and move beyond the challenges they face.

His experience of defying the odds stretches beyond overcoming personal challenges and into the business realm. Growing up, Chris worked in the family "startup" business. That startup went on to gross over $200 million. In the years since, Chris has started or had ownership in over 10 businesses, experiencing a wide range of ups and downs, from losing everything to building it all back from scratch.

While serving as CMO at Oven Bits, he drove over 100% growth adding millions in revenue and helping to produce 20+ features in the Apple and Google app stores. This was done in partnership with brands such as L'Oréal, Lush Cosmetics, Hilton, and Vogue. During this time, Chris published his first book, **Step:** *Pursuing Your Dreams in the Midst of Everyday Life.*

Chris has since produced **Life Story:** *A Step-by-Step Guide to Creating the Life You've Always Wanted*, **The "Blank" Leader:** *An In-Depth Guide to Becoming a Thriving Leader*, **The Intentional Year:** *A Year Dedicated to Making You Unstoppable*, **Shaping Belief** and **#Goals**.

Through the exhilarating heights of hard-earned success to the lows of disappointing failures, Chris has learned a handful of key principles that have helped him defeat the odds. He's now on a mission to teach people of all walks of life how they can do the same and defeat the odds no matter what their "everyday life" looks like.

Find all of Chris' resources at ChrisCapehart.co.

www.ingramcontent.com/pod-product-compliance
Lightning Source LLC
Chambersburg PA
CBHW050456110426
42743CB00017B/3389